Rough Country Trading Post
P. O. Box 127
Dinosaur, Colorado 81610.
Wagner, John

Hilarious Horses, 2nd ed.
March 21, 2015

Book design by John A Wagner
Photographs by John A Wagner

More Adventures… by John Wagner

First Flight- Journey of a Man and an Eagle

The Magnificent Wild Mustangs of Sand Wash Basin

Picasso: Wild Stallion of the West

The Bird Herd of Sand Wash Basin

Fighting Stallions of Sand Wash Basin

Frightfull Freefall's Photo Album

Foxy Foxes

Rock Art & Ruins of Northwestern Colorado and Northeastern Utah

The Legend of Jericho Jones

Run Son, Run Series

Run Son, Run

Run Son, Run part 2

Run Son, Run part 3

To Boldly Go Where No Horses Has Gone Before part 4

To Boldly Go Where No Horses Has Gone Before part 5

Sand Wash Basin lies in Northwestern Colorado. This is where the wild horses roam on 163,000 acres of blm, state and private land.

The area is so huge that sometimes small bands of wild horses are hard to find. I've talked to different people that said, "We drove all day and only found one horse!" "Where are they hiding at?"

I smile and say. "Playing Hide & Seek."

Happy Trails
John

Hilarious Horses
by
John A Wagner

"Lookout Everyone, John's here with that clicky thing again!"

"Great Jumping Jackrabbits, what in the world are you doing, John?"

"Don't you dare take my picture? Did I hear a click?"

"Bug in the ear!"

"It's a Bird!"

"It's a Plane!"

"It's John in an Airplane."

"I see him. What's John doing up there?"

"All Photographers do is click, click, and click. Yup, yup, yup."

"Home Sweet Home, where you can scratch where it itches."

"Can you do this?"

"YIKES! It's a Spideeeeer!"

"Psssst, John's here!"

"Whoa! Look at the size of that Stink Bug!"

"The secret of splashing is to do it this way!"
"Ha-ha. You're all wet!"

"Is that what I think it is?"

"I knew it…I knew it…You can't hide a camera from me!"

"Great Gobs of Toads, I almost stepped on a Horny Toad!"
"Smashing Toads with your hooves is seven years of bad luck!"

"I'm practicing Howling. I'll fool those coyotes tonight. Ha-ha!"

The little foal Fury has an attitude.

"Oh my, I hope the horse apples don't drop now!"

"Ha-ha! Nobody can see me now!"

Some days I just feel like a nut.

**John Wagner lives in Dinosaur, Colorado with his wife
Sarah, daughter Megan and their dog Buddy.
John loves the great outdoors and photography is his hobby.**